EASY JAM COOKBOOK

THE EFFORTLESS CHEF SERIES

2nd Edition

By
Chef Maggie Chow
Copyright © 2015 by Saxonberg
Associates
All rights reserved

Published by
BookSumo, a division of Saxonberg
Associates
http://www.booksumo.com/

Stay To the End of the Cookbook and Receive....

I really appreciate when people, take the time to read all of my recipes.

So, as a gift for reading this entire cookbook you will receive a **massive collection of special recipes.**

Read to the end of this cookbook and get my ***Easy Specialty Cookbook Box Set for FREE***!

This box set includes the following:

1. *Easy Sushi Cookbook*

2. ***Easy Dump Dinner Cookbook***
3. ***Easy Beans Cookbook***

Remember this box set is about **EASY** cooking.

In the ***Easy Sushi Cookbook*** you will learn the easiest methods to prepare almost every type of Japanese Sushi i.e. *California Rolls, the Perfect Sushi Rice, Crab Rolls, Osaka Style Sushi*, and so many others.

Then we go on to *Dump Dinners*. Nothing can be easier than a Dump Dinner. In the ***Easy Dump Dinner Cookbook*** we will learn how to master our slow cookers and make some amazingly unique dinners that will take almost ***no effort***.

Finally in the ***Easy Beans Cookbook*** we tackle one of my favorite side dishes: Beans. There are so many delicious ways to make Baked Beans and Bean Salads that I had to share them.

So stay till the end and then keep on cooking with my *Easy Specialty Cookbook Box Set*!

ABOUT THE AUTHOR.

Maggie Chow is the author and creator of your favorite *Easy Cookbooks* and *The Effortless Chef Series*. Maggie is a lover of all things related to food. Maggie loves nothing more than finding new recipes, trying them out, and then making them her own, by adding or removing ingredients, tweaking cooking times, and anything to make the recipe not only taste better, but be easier to cook!

For a complete listing of all my books please see my author page.

INTRODUCTION

Welcome to *The Effortless Chef Series*! Thank you for taking the time to download the *Easy Jamaican Cookbook*. Come take a journey with me into the delights of easy cooking. The point of this cookbook and all my cookbooks is to exemplify the effortless nature of cooking simply.

In this book we focus on Jamaican and West Indian cuisines. You will find that even though the recipes are simple, the taste of the dishes is quite amazing.

So will you join me in an adventure of simple cooking? If the answer is yes (and I hope it is) please consult the table of contents to find the dishes you are most interested in. Once you are ready jump right in and start cooking.

— Chef Maggie Chow

TABLE OF CONTENTS

STAY TO THE END OF THE COOKBOOK AND RECEIVE.. 2
About the Author.................................. 5
Introduction 7
Table of Contents 8
Any Issues? Contact Me 12
Legal Notes.. 13
Chapter 1: Easy Jamaican Recipes...... 14
    Jerk Chicken I 14
    Cabbage Jamaican Style................... 17
    Beef Patties I 20
    Burgers In Jamaica 23
    Caribbean Rice................................. 26
    Oxtail 29
    A Caribbean Soup of Spinach 32
    Kingston Curry Chicken 35

Jamaican Bread 38
Jerk Seasoning 42
Snapper Deep Fried 45
Curry Chicken I 48
Ten Speed 51
(Party Drink) 51
Maggie's Favorite Burrito 52
(Jerk Tofu) 52
A Caribbean Soup of Tortilla 55
Slow Cooker Caribbean Sandwich ... 58
Chicken and Rice 62
Jamaican Wings 65
Jerk Sauce 68
Jerk Chicken II 71
Montego Bay Chicken 74
Beef Patties II 77
Dumplings 81
Easier Jamaican Curry Chicken 84
Jamaican Bread II 87
(Banana) 87

Jamaican Pork 91
Caribbean Cranberry Spread........... 94
Shrimp Kebabs................................. 96
Caribbean Style Fettuccine.............. 99
Fruity Rum Cake 102
West Indian Egg Noodle Low Mein
.... 105
Jamaican Wings II 108
Sweet and Spicy Wings 112
Cod Fritters.................................... 115
Jamaican Pastries 118
Maggie's Easy Caribbean Lime Mahi Mahi.. 122
West Indian Potatoes 125
West Indian Hot Habanero Sauce . 129
Bok Choy from Trinidad................ 132
Caribbean Stew 135
Port of Spain Chicken.................... 138
Spanish Caribbean Beef 141
Jamaican Salad 144
Shrimp Salad 148

Spicy Coconut Chicken Bake 150

Trinidad Chicken and Curry 153

Caribbean Rice 156

Pina Colada 159

Fried Conch 161

Brown Rice XXXI 164

(Easy Jamaican Style) 164

THANKS FOR READING! NOW LET'S TRY SOME **SUSHI** AND **DUMP DINNERS** 167

Come On... 169

Let's Be Friends :) 169

Can I Ask A Favour? 170

Interested in Other Easy Cookbooks? 171

Any Issues? Contact Me

If you find that something important to you is missing from this book please contact me at <u>maggie@booksumo.com</u>.

I will try my best to re-publish a revised copy taking your feedback into consideration and let you know when the book has been revised with you in mind.

:)

— Chef Maggie Chow

LEGAL NOTES

ALL RIGHTS RESERVED. NO PART OF THIS BOOK MAY BE REPRODUCED OR TRANSMITTED IN ANY FORM OR BY ANY MEANS. PHOTOCOPYING, POSTING ONLINE, AND / OR DIGITAL COPYING IS STRICTLY PROHIBITED UNLESS WRITTEN PERMISSION IS GRANTED BY THE BOOK'S PUBLISHING COMPANY. LIMITED USE OF THE BOOK'S TEXT IS PERMITTED FOR USE IN REVIEWS WRITTEN FOR THE PUBLIC AND/OR PUBLIC DOMAIN.

Chapter 1: Easy Jamaican Recipes

Jerk Chicken I

Ingredients:

- 1/2 green onion, minced
- 1/4 C. orange juice
- 1 tbsp minced fresh ginger root
- 1 tbsp minced jalapeno peppers
- 1 tbsp lime juice
- 1 tbsp soy sauce
- 1 clove garlic, minced
- 1 tsp ground allspice
- 1/4 tsp ground cinnamon
- 1/2 tsp ground cloves
- 1 (2 to 3 lb) whole chicken, cut into pieces

Directions:

- For marinade mix the following evenly: cloves, onions, cinnamon, orange juice, allspice, ginger, garlic, pepper, soy sauce, and lemon juice.
- Cover your chicken with the marinade. Place lid on the container. Put everything in the frig for 7 to 8 hrs.
- Get a grill hot. Grill the chicken until fully done, time depends on heat level. 7-8 mins each side. Boil extra marinade for 5 mins and use as a coating or discard.
- Enjoy.

NOTE: Traditional jerk chicken in Jamaica is prepared with an open flame.

Servings: 4

Timing Information:

Preparation	Cooking	Total Time
10 mins	20 mins	8 hrs 30 mins

Nutritional Information:

Calories	834 kcal
Carbohydrates	4.8 g
Cholesterol	284 mg
Fat	57.2 g
Fiber	0.6 g
Protein	71.1 g
Sodium	568 mg

* Percent Daily Values are based on a 2,000 calorie diet.

Cabbage Jamaican Style

Ingredients:

- 1 head cabbage
- 2 tbsps olive oil, or as needed
- 1 small onion, thinly sliced
- 1/2 chopped green bell pepper
- 1 green onion, sliced
- 2 sprigs fresh thyme
- 1 whole Scotch bonnet chili pepper
- 1 tsp salt (optional)
- 1 C. shredded carrots
- 1/4 C. white vinegar
- 2 tbsps white sugar

Directions:

- Remove the core of the cabbage, remove outside leaves, and dice the cabbage into pieces.
- Get a frying pan. Get some olive oil hot. Stir fry green onion, and

green peppers for 5 mins. Add salt, bonnet pepper, and thyme into the onions, and keep stirring.
- Add carrots and cabbage to the pan. Place a lid on the pan. Set heat to low. Cook for 10 mins.
- Mix in sugar and vinegar. Cover. Let it cook for 3 additional mins.
- Throw away thyme pieces and bonnet peppers. Let cool.
- Enjoy.

Servings: 6

Timing Information:

Preparation	Cooking	Total Time
20 mins	20 mins	40 mins

Nutritional Information:

Calories	121 kcal
Carbohydrates	19.2 g
Cholesterol	0 mg
Fat	4.8 g
Fiber	5.9 g
Protein	3 g
Sodium	437 mg

* Percent Daily Values are based on a 2,000 calorie diet.

BEEF PATTIES I

Ingredients:

- 3 lbs lean ground beef
- 2 C. seasoned bread crumbs
- 1 (28 oz.) can tomato sauce
- 1 bunch (1-inch) pieces green onions
- 1/4 C. soy sauce
- 1/4 C. Maggi™ liquid seasoning
- 1 tbsp salt
- 1 tbsp pepper
- 1 tsp vinegar-based hot pepper sauce
- 2 recipes pie crust pastry
- 2 eggs
- 1/4 C. water

Directions:

- Get a big bowl. Combine the following: hot sauce, ground beef, pepper, bread crumbs, salt,

tomato sauce, Maggi seasoning, soy sauce, and green onions.
- Mix evenly with two spoons, or use hands.
- Heat your oven to 425 degrees.
- Flatten pie dough to 1/8 an inch, make six circles. Add a tbsp of filling to the middle of each.
- Fold dough into a semi-circle and press down on the outside edge to seal.
- Freeze patties for later use or lightly coat them with whisked eggs and put them in the oven for 40 mins.

NOTE: If the pie is fresh from the freezer then add 10 more mins in the oven.

Servings: 36

Timing Information:

Preparation	Cooking	Total Time
25 mins	40 mins	1 hr 5 mins

Nutritional Information:

Calories	215 kcal
Carbohydrates	15.6 g
Cholesterol	33 mg
Fat	12.5 g
Fiber	1.6 g
Protein	9.9 g
Sodium	667 mg

* Percent Daily Values are based on a 2,000 calorie diet.

BURGERS IN JAMAICA

Ingredients:

- 2 tbsps olive oil
- 2 1/4 C. chopped onion
- 3 cloves garlic, minced
- 1 habanero pepper, chopped
- 1 1/2 tbsps grated fresh ginger root
- 1 tsp salt
- 3/4 tsp ground allspice
- 3/4 tsp ground nutmeg
- 2 1/4 C. cooked black beans, rinsed and drained
- 2 1/4 C. cooked long-grain white rice
- 2 1/2 C. dry bread crumbs
- 6 hamburger buns, split

Directions:

- Get a frying pan and get 1 tbsp of olive hot. Stir fry garlic and onions for 4 mins.
- Combine habanero and keep stir frying until everything is soft. Set aside in a bowl.
- In the same bowl, mix, with your hands: bread crumbs, rice, and beans. Season with: nutmeg, ginger, salt, and allspice.
- Shape into burgers.
- Heat oil again in frying pan and fry your burgers for 10 mins.
- Add buns and enjoy.

Servings: 6

Timing Information:

Preparation	Cooking	Total Time
2 mins	15 mins	17 mins

Nutritional Information:

Calories	531 kcal
Carbohydrates	92.6 g
Cholesterol	0 mg
Fat	9.7 g
Fiber	10.9 g
Protein	17.5 g
Sodium	1307 mg

* Percent Daily Values are based on a 2,000 calorie diet.

Caribbean Rice

Ingredients:

- 1 tbsp vegetable oil
- 1/2 large onion, sliced
- 1/2 red apple, cored and sliced
- 1 pinch curry powder
- 1 C. water
- 2/3 C. brown rice
- 1 tsp dark molasses or treacle
- 1 small banana, sliced
- 1 tbsp unsweetened flaked coconut

Directions:

- Get a saucepan. With medium heat, get your oil hot.
- Stir fry apples and onions until the onions are translucent. Combine your curry and water.
- Get the water boiling and then mix in rice and molasses. Place a

lid on the pan. Set heat to low. Cook for 30 mins.
- Add banana, and garnish with coconut.
- Enjoy.

Servings: 2

Timing Information:

Preparation	Cooking	Total Time
15 mins	30 mins	45 mins

Nutritional Information:

Calories	398 kcal
Carbohydrates	71.6 g
Cholesterol	0 mg
Fat	10.7 g
Fiber	5.6 g
Protein	6.1 g
Sodium	11 mg

* Percent Daily Values are based on a 2,000 calorie diet.

Oxtail

Ingredients:

- 1 lb beef oxtail, cut into pieces
- 1 large onion, chopped
- 1 green onion, thinly sliced
- 2 cloves garlic, minced
- 1 tsp minced fresh ginger root
- 1 scotch bonnet chili pepper, chopped
- 2 tbsps soy sauce
- 1 sprig fresh thyme, chopped
- 1/2 tsp salt
- 1 tsp black pepper
- 2 tbsps vegetable oil
- 1 1/2 C. water
- 1 C. canned fava beans, drained
- 1 tsp whole allspice berries
- 1 tbsp cornstarch
- 2 tbsps water

Directions:

- Get a bowl. Combine the following: pepper, onion, green onion, salt, garlic, thyme, ginger, chili pepper.
- Add oxtail to the bowl. Toss to coat.
- Get a frying pan. Get veggie oil hot. Stir fry oxtails and seasoning for 10 mins.
- Place oxtail in a pressure cooker with one and a half C. of water. Pressure cook oxtails for 25 mins.
- Combine allspice berries, and fava beans in your frying pan. Heat until lightly boiling. Mix in 2 tbsps of water and mix cornstarch in. Add oxtails to cornstarch. Keep everything simmering until sauce is thick.

Servings: 4

Timing Information:

Preparation	Cooking	Total Time
30 mins	45 mins	1 hr 15 mins

Nutritional Information:

Calories	425 kcal
Carbohydrates	17.6 g
Cholesterol	125 mg
Fat	22.4 g
Fiber	3.7 g
Protein	38.8 g
Sodium	1089 mg

* Percent Daily Values are based on a 2,000 calorie diet.

A Caribbean Soup of Spinach

Ingredients:

- 3 tbsps olive oil
- 1 onion, chopped
- 2 stalks celery, chopped
- 4 cloves garlic, minced
- 2 tbsps fresh ginger root, minced
- 1 tbsp sugar
- 2 tsps sea salt
- 1/4 tsp ground turmeric
- 1/4 tsp ground allspice
- 1/4 tsp ground nutmeg
- 2 potatoes, peeled and diced
- 4 C. chopped zucchini
- 6 C. vegetable stock
- 1 pinch cayenne pepper
- 1 C. chopped fresh spinach
- 1/2 red bell pepper, minced

Directions:

- Get a frying pan. Get your oil hot. Stir fry sugar, onion, ginger, and celery for 5 mins.
- Combine in salt, nutmeg, allspice, and turmeric, mix evenly. Add zucchini, and potatoes, and veggie stock.
- Heat everything until boiling. Set heat to low. Let everything lightly boil for 10 mins. Set everything aside.
- Combine in spinach and cayenne, mix until even.
- Add bell pepper.
- Enjoy.

Servings: 8

Timing Information:

Preparation	Cooking	Total Time
30 mins	20 mins	50 mins

Nutritional Information:

Calories	124 kcal
Carbohydrates	16.7 g
Cholesterol	0 mg
Fat	5.8 g
Fiber	2.6 g
Protein	2.6 g
Sodium	667 mg

* Percent Daily Values are based on a 2,000 calorie diet.

Kingston Curry Chicken

Ingredients:

- 1/4 C. curry powder, divided
- 2 tbsps garlic powder
- 1 tbsp seasoned salt
- 1 tbsp onion powder
- 2 tsps salt
- 1 sprig fresh thyme, leaves stripped
- 1 pinch ground allspice, or more to taste
- salt and ground black pepper to taste
- 2 1/4 lbs whole chicken, cut into pieces
- 3 tbsps vegetable oil
- 3 C. water
- 1 potato, diced
- 1/2 C. chopped carrots
- 2 scallions (green onions), chopped
- 1 (1 inch) piece fresh ginger root, minced

- 1 Scotch bonnet chili pepper, chopped, or to taste

Directions:

- Get a bowl and combine the following: pepper, 2 tbsps curry, salt, garlic powder, allspice, seasoned salt, thyme, onion powder.
- Cover your chicken with the dry seasoning evenly.
- Get a frying pan. Get 2 tbsps of curry and oil hot. Heat for 2 mins.
- Mix in in chicken. Set heat to medium and combine carrot, water, potato, chili pepper, ginger, and scallions.
- Place a lid on pan and let chicken simmer for 40 mins. Temp should be 165 degrees. Set chicken aside. Let the gravy get thicker if you like, by continuing to heat, otherwise serve.
- Enjoy.

Servings: 6

Timing Information:

Preparation	Cooking	Total Time
20 mins	30 mins	50 mins

Nutritional Information:

Calories	348 kcal
Carbohydrates	13.8 g
Cholesterol	103 mg
Fat	20.3 g
Fiber	3.1 g
Protein	27.8 g
Sodium	1353 mg

* Percent Daily Values are based on a 2,000 calorie diet.

Jamaican Bread

Ingredients:

- 3 1/4 C. all-purpose flour
- 4 tsps baking powder
- 2 tsps ground cinnamon
- 1 tsp ground nutmeg
- 1/2 tsp ground allspice
- 1 pinch salt
- 1 egg
- 1 C. milk
- 1/3 C. beer
- 1 3/4 C. brown sugar
- 1/2 C. melted butter
- 1 tsp browning sauce
- 1 tsp vanilla extract
- 1 tsp lime juice
- 1 C. raisins

Icing:

- 1/2 C. brown sugar
- 1/2 C. water

Directions:

- Get your oven hot to 325 degrees.
- Get two bread loaf baking dishes coat them with nonstick spray or oil.
- Get a bowl. Whisk the following: salt, flour, allspice, baking powder, nutmeg, and cinnamon.
- Get another bowl. Whisk eggs, beer, one and 3/4 C. brown sugar, and milk evenly.
- To the wet mixture add butter, lime juice, browning sauce, and vanilla extract. Combine some raisins and then combine both bowls.
- Evenly mix until completely smooth.
- Fill baking pans with mixture, bake for 1 hour.
- Before everything is done. Get a saucepan to make the glaze. Add 1/2 C. brown sugar, and water. Simmer / boil until it becomes a glaze, about 5 mins.
- Let it cool for 4 mins then when everything is finished baking coat with glaze.

Servings: 20

Timing Information:

Preparation	Cooking	Total Time
25 mins	1 hr 5 mins	2 hrs 30 mins

Nutritional Information:

Calories	245 kcal
Carbohydrates	46.9 g
Cholesterol	22 mg
Fat	5.4 g
Fiber	1 g
Protein	3.2 g
Sodium	147 mg

* Percent Daily Values are based on a 2,000 calorie diet.

JERK SEASONING

Ingredients:

- 1 1/2 C. allspice
- 8 C. salt
- 5 1/2 C. garlic powder
- 4 C. white sugar
- 1 C. chipotle chili powder
- 1/2 C. ground cloves
- 2 C. dried thyme leaves
- 2 C. ground black pepper
- 4 C. cayenne pepper
- 1 C. ground cinnamon

Directions:

- Get a bowl. Combine all the spices very evenly.
- Use something airtight for continually storage and freshness.

- For every serving of meat. Use one and a half tsps of this mix for seasoning.
- It will take about an hour of marinating time for best tastes.

NOTE: This is very important for other recipes which call for jerk seasoning. Please use this one.

Servings: 26

Timing Information:

Preparation	Cooking	Total Time
15 mins		15 mins

Nutritional Information:

Calories	10 kcal
Carbohydrates	2.4 g
Cholesterol	0 mg
Fat	0.1 g
Fiber	0.5 g
Protein	0.3 g
Sodium	1074 mg

* Percent Daily Values are based on a 2,000 calorie diet.

Snapper Deep Fried

Ingredients:

- 1 (1 1/2 lb) whole red snapper, cleaned and scaled
- salt and pepper, according to preference
- 1 quart vegetable oil
- 1 tsp vegetable oil
- 1/2 white onion, sliced
- 1/8 tsp minced garlic
- 1/2 large carrot, peeled and cut into thin strips
- 1 sprig fresh thyme, leaves stripped
- 1 allspice berry, cracked
- 1/4 habanero pepper, seeded and minced
- 1/4 C. white vinegar
- 1 tbsp water
- 3/4 tsp salt
- 1 pinch brown sugar

Directions:

- Take your fish and make three long length-wise cuts. Coat with pepper and salt.
- Get a frying pan. Get 1 qt. of oil hot and ready for frying.
- Once oil is hot, fry fish for 5 mins per side. Set aside on paper towel after fried fully.
- Get another frying pan and get 1 tsp of oil hot.
- Stir fry in the 2nd pan: carrots, onion, and garlic for 3 mins.
- For 5 mins stir fry the following with onions: sugar, allspice, salt, habaneros, water, and vinegar.
- Use contents of 2nd pan as a coating for your fish.
- Enjoy.

Servings: 1

Timing Information:

Preparation	Cooking	Total Time
10 mins	15 mins	25 mins

Nutritional Information:

Calories	770 kcal
Carbohydrates	4.9 g
Cholesterol	125 mg
Fat	50.9 g
Fiber	1 g
Protein	70.3 g
Sodium	1036 mg

* Percent Daily Values are based on a 2,000 calorie diet.

Curry Chicken I

Ingredients:

- 1/4 C. vegetable oil
- 1 onion, chopped
- 1 tomato, chopped
- 1 garlic clove, chopped
- 2 tbsps Jamaican-style curry powder
- 2 slices habanero pepper (optional)
- 1/4 tsp ground thyme
- 2 skinless, boneless chicken breast halves, cut into 1 1/2-inch pieces
- 1 C. water
- 1/2 tsp salt, or to taste

Directions:

- Get a frying pan. Get veggie oil hot.

- Stir fry habaneros, onion, thyme, tomato, curry powder, and garlic for 7 mins. Add chicken and fry for 5 mins.
- Add water to the onions and chicken, and set heat to low. Place a lid on pan. Let everything lightly boil for 30 mins.
- Enjoy.

Servings: 4

Timing Information:

Preparation	Cooking	Total Time
10 mins	45 mins	55 mins

Nutritional Information:

Calories	210 kcal
Carbohydrates	6.2 g
Cholesterol	30 mg
Fat	15.4 g
Fiber	2 g
Protein	12.5 g
Sodium	322 mg

* Percent Daily Values are based on a 2,000 calorie diet.

TEN SPEED

(PARTY DRINK)

Ingredients:

- 1 fluid oz. melon liqueur
- 1 fluid oz. vodka
- 1 fluid oz. coconut flavored rum
- 3 fluid oz. cranberry juice
- 3 fluid oz. pineapple juice

Directions:

- Combine all the ingredients into a cocktail shaker. Sieve or strain contents into a martini glass.
- Serve chilled.

NOTE: Please drink responsibly.

Maggie's Favorite Burrito

(Jerk Tofu)

Ingredients:

- 3/4 C. jerk marinade
- 5 tbsps lime juice
- 2 cloves garlic, diced
- 1 pinch ground black pepper, or to taste
- 2 C. pressed tofu, diced
- Nonstick spray
- 2 C. diced jicama
- 1 C. diced pineapple
- 2 C. cooked rice
- 1 (15 oz.) can black beans, drained
- 8 flour tortillas
- 1/2 C. shredded Monterey Jack cheese
- 1/2 C. salsa
- 1/2 C. sour cream

Directions:

- Get a bowl. Mix the following: garlic, half C. marinade, black pepper, one 1/4 C. lime juice. Put everything in a Ziploc bag with tofu. Put in the frig for 30 mins.
- Remove marinade. Get a frying pan, coat with nonstick spray. Stir -fry tofu with medium heat for 4 mins. Set aside in a bowl.
- Stir fry 1/4 C. marinade, jicama, 1 tbsp lime juice, and pineapple for 2.5 mins. Add tofu fry for another 2.5 mins.
- Each tortilla should have 1/3 C. of tofu, and some rice and beans. Roll to form a burrito.
- Garnish with sour cream and salsa.
- Enjoy.

Servings: 8

Timing Information:

Preparation	Cooking	Total Time
20 mins	10 mins	1 hr

Nutritional Information:

Calories	386 kcal
Carbohydrates	58.4 g
Cholesterol	13 mg
Fat	11 g
Fiber	7.4 g
Protein	17 g
Sodium	1243 mg

* Percent Daily Values are based on a 2,000 calorie diet.

A Caribbean Soup of Tortilla

Ingredients:

- 3 skinless, boneless chicken breast halves
- 8 C. water
- 8 tsps chicken bouillon granules
- 1 C. chopped carrot
- 1/4 tsp ground allspice
- 1/2 tsp chopped fresh thyme
- 1/8 tsp ground cinnamon
- 1 tbsp chopped fresh ginger
- 1 tbsp minced garlic
- 1 C. chopped tomato
- 1 C. coconut milk
- 1 tsp hot pepper sauce
- 1 C. shredded mozzarella cheese
- 2 C. crispy tortilla strips
- 2 limes, cut into wedges

Directions:

- Grill chicken breast for 8 mins on each side on a grill or grilling plate. Dice into cubes.
- Get a big pot. Add water, chicken, carrots, and bouillon. Add the following spices: garlic, allspice, ginger, cinnamon, and thyme. Get it boiling then lower heat to medium. Let everything lightly boil for 10 min.
- Combine coconut milk, tomato, and pepper sauce. Let cook for 2 more mins.
- Divide soup into bowls. Garnish with mozzarella and julienned tortilla, and some lime pieces.

Servings: 8

Timing Information:

Preparation	Cooking	Total Time
20 mins	20 mins	40 mins

Nutritional Information:

Calories	196 kcal
Carbohydrates	10.6 g
Cholesterol	35 mg
Fat	11.3 g
Fiber	1.9 g
Protein	14.6 g
Sodium	540 mg

* Percent Daily Values are based on a 2,000 calorie diet.

Slow Cooker Caribbean Sandwich

Ingredients:

Pulled Turkey:

- 1/2 C. chopped celery
- 1/3 C. chopped green onion
- 1 (2 lb) skinless, boneless turkey breast, cut into 8 oz. chunks
- 1/2 C. juice from canned pineapple
- 1/4 C. sweet chile sauce
- 3 tbsps distilled white vinegar
- 2 tbsps water
- 1 tbsp beef bouillon granules
- 2 tsps garlic powder
- 6 canned pineapple rings

Coleslaw Topping:

- 1/4 C. mayonnaise
- 1 tbsp lemon juice
- 2 tbsps chopped fresh parsley
- 1/2 C. chopped onion

- 2 C. chopped cabbage
- 1 C. shredded Cheddar cheese
- salt and black pepper to taste
- 6 Kaiser rolls, split

Directions:

- Put onions and celery in your slow cooker. Then layer turkey on top.
- Then season with the following: beef bouillon, pineapple juice, garlic powder, vinegar, sweet chili sauce, and water.
- Garnish turkey with pineapple rings (the topmost layer).
- Turn on slow cooker to lowest setting for 7 hours.
- Get a bowl combine the following: onion, mayo, parsley, and lemon juice. Mix evenly.
- Add cheddar, cabbage, salt and pepper. Put into the frig for 5 hours or while slow cooker is going.

- After 7 hours, break apart the turkey with a utensil.
- Put turkey on a roll with coleslaw too.
- Enjoy.

Servings: 6

Timing Information:

Preparation	Cooking	Total Time
35 mins	6 hrs	6 hrs 35 mins

Nutritional Information:

Calories	524 kcal
Carbohydrates	42.8 g
Cholesterol	133 mg
Fat	16.5 g
Fiber	3.1 g
Protein	49.4 g
Sodium	808 mg

* Percent Daily Values are based on a 2,000 calorie diet.

Chicken and Rice

Ingredients:

- 1/2 C. uncooked long-grain white rice
- 1 C. water
- 3 tbsps vegetable oil
- 1/4 C. butter
- 3 skinless, boneless chicken breast halves
- 3 fluid oz. dark rum
- 1 (6 oz.) can broiled-in-butter-style sliced mushrooms
- 2 1/2 tbsps chicken bouillon granules
- 2 tsps garlic powder
- 2 tsps ground black pepper
- 1 (14 oz.) can coconut milk
- 1 small banana, sliced

Directions:

- Get a saucepan. Bring water and rice to boil. Set heat to low. Let everything cook for 24 mins.
- Get a frying pan. Heat oil and butter. Stir fry chicken for 7 mins on each side.
- Cover chicken with rum. Get a match and set the rum on fire (be careful please). Let the flames burn out.
- Combine in the following: coconut milk, mushrooms, pepper, garlic powder, and bouillon. Set heat to low. Cook for 11 mins.
- Enjoy chicken and mushrooms with some rice.

Servings: 3

Timing Information:

Preparation	Cooking	Total Time
15 mins	30 mins	45 mins

Nutritional Information:

Calories	916 kcal
Carbohydrates	42.9 g
Cholesterol	113 mg
Fat	61.9 g
Fiber	3.7 g
Protein	34.8 g
Sodium	1322 mg

* Percent Daily Values are based on a 2,000 calorie diet.

Jamaican Wings

Ingredients:

- 3 tbsps Jamaican jerk seasoning blend
- 3 tbsps vegetable oil
- 3 cloves garlic, diced
- 1 (1 inch) piece peeled fresh ginger, diced
- 1 bunch green onions, chopped
- 12 slices pickled jalapeno peppers
- 4 lbs chicken wings

Directions:

- Get your blender and mix the following until smooth and even: jalapeno pieces, jerk seasoning, onions, oil, ginger, and garlic.
- Coat wings with this sauce. Cover the container of wings and sauce. Put everything in the frig throughout the night.

- Bake wings in 300 degree preheated oven for 2 hrs.
- Enjoy.

Servings: 8

Timing Information:

Preparation	Cooking	Total Time
25 mins	2 hrs	10 hrs 25 mins

Nutritional Information:

Calories	230 kcal
Carbohydrates	4.4 g
Cholesterol	48 mg
Fat	16.4 g
Fiber	1.5 g
Protein	16 g
Sodium	647 mg

* Percent Daily Values are based on a 2,000 calorie diet.

Jerk Sauce

Ingredients:

- 1 bunch green onions, chopped
- 1/2 C. peanut oil
- 1/2 C. vinegar
- 3 tbsps ground allspice
- 3 habanero peppers
- 1 (1 inch) piece fresh ginger, peeled
- 5 cloves garlic, peeled
- 2 limes, juiced
- 1/4 C. dark brown sugar
- 2 tbsps chopped fresh thyme
- 2 tbsps soy sauce
- 2 tbsps ketchup
- 1 tbsp whole black peppercorns
- 1 tbsp ground cinnamon

Directions:

- Very simple to make this version of jerk sauce. Get your blender and blend all the ingredients together until very smooth. Store in air tight containers preferably, but, jars will do as well.

NOTE: Make sure to keep this refrigerated.

Servings: 4

Timing Information:

Preparation	Cooking	Total Time
15 mins		15 mins

Nutritional Information:

Calories	354 kcal
Carbohydrates	29.2 g
Cholesterol	0 mg
Fat	27.7 g
Fiber	4.3 g
Protein	2.6 g
Sodium	553 mg

* Percent Daily Values are based on a 2,000 calorie diet.

JERK CHICKEN II

Ingredients:

- 6 skinless, boneless chicken breast halves - cut into chunks
- 4 limes, juiced
- 1 C. water
- 2 tsps ground allspice
- 1/2 tsp ground nutmeg
- 1 tsp salt
- 1 tsp brown sugar
- 2 tsps dried thyme
- 1 tsp ground ginger
- 1 1/2 tsps ground black pepper
- 2 tbsps vegetable oil
- 2 onions, chopped
- 1 1/2 C. chopped green onions
- 6 cloves garlic, chopped
- 2 habanero peppers, chopped

Directions:

- Get a bowl. Put in water and lime juice. Put in your chicken. Make sure it is covered. Set to the side.
- Get a blender. Blend the following until smooth: black pepper, allspice, veggie oil, thyme, nutmeg, ginger, brown sugar, and salt.
- Continue blending after adding onions, habaneros, green onions, and garlic. Get everything smooth.
- Mix blender contents with your chicken. Leave a bit for basting. Cover the chicken with lid and put in the frig for 3 hours.
- Get a grill, coated with oil, hot.
- Grill your chicken until fully cooked making sure to cover with additional marinade that was placed to the side. (The marinade that soaked the chicken should be discarded.)
- Move and flip chicken often during grilling time.
- Enjoy.

Servings: 6

Timing Information:

Preparation	Cooking	Total Time
20 mins	1 hr	3 hrs 20 mins

Nutritional Information:

Calories	221 kcal
Carbohydrates	13.3 g
Cholesterol	68 mg
Fat	6.4 g
Fiber	3.2 g
Protein	28.8 g
Sodium	474 mg

* Percent Daily Values are based on a 2,000 calorie diet.

.

Montego Bay Chicken

Ingredients:

- 1 large red onion
- 3 cloves garlic
- 1 habanero pepper, seeded
- 1 tbsp fresh ginger root
- 1/4 C. olive oil
- 1/4 C. brown sugar
- 3 tbsps red wine vinegar
- 3 tbsps orange juice concentrate, thawed
- 1 tsp soy sauce
- 2 tsps ground cinnamon
- 1/2 tsp ground nutmeg
- 1/4 tsp ground cloves
- 1/2 C. chopped cilantro
- 1/2 tsp salt and pepper to taste
- 6 skinless, boneless chicken breast halves

Directions:

- Get your food processor. Pulse until the following until minced: ginger, onion, habaneros, and garlic.
- Combine the following in the process: pepper, olive oil, salt, brown sugar, cilantro, vinegar, cloves, concentrated orange juice, nutmeg, cinnamon and soy sauce. Pulse some more. This is your marinade.
- Cover chicken with marinade, place a lid on the container. Put everything in the frig throughout the night.
- Heat oil grill.
- Chicken should grilled for 10 mins on each side.
- Enjoy.

NOTE: Discard remaining marinade.

Servings: 6

Timing Information:

Preparation	Cooking	Total Time
30 mins	30 mins	1 day 1 hr

Nutritional Information:

Calories	279 kcal
Carbohydrates	17 g
Cholesterol	67 mg
Fat	12 g
Fiber	1.2 g
Protein	25.3 g
Sodium	309 mg

* Percent Daily Values are based on a 2,000 calorie diet.

Beef Patties II

Ingredients:

- 2 C. all-purpose flour
- 1 1/2 tsps curry powder
- 1 dash salt
- 1/4 C. margarine
- 1/4 C. shortening
- 1/3 C. water
- 2 tbsps margarine
- 1 lb ground beef
- 1 small onion, finely diced
- 1 tsp curry powder
- 1 tsp dried thyme
- 1 tsp salt
- 1 tsp pepper
- 1/2 C. beef broth
- 1/2 C. dry bread crumbs
- 1 egg, beaten

Directions:

- Get oven hot to 400 degrees.

- Get a bowl and mix the following: salt, 1.5 tsps curry powder, and flour.
- Combine also to form crumbs: 1/4 C. shortening and margarine.
- Form a ball-like shape by adding water.
- Flatten the ball into a cylinder.
- Slice the cylinder into 10 parts. Flatten each part into a circle. Set to the side.
- Get a frying pan hot with more margarine. Stir fry onions until see-through and stir-fry your beef.
- Season beef with the following: pepper, 1 tsp curry, thyme, and 1 tsp salt.
- Stir fry everything until beef is cooked. Then add bread crumps and broth. Lower heat and let contents simmer until no liquid is left.
- Fill each dough circle with beef and fold into a semi-circle. Flatten the edge with a utensil.

Coat the top of each patty with some whisked egg.
- Bake in oven for 30 mins.

Servings: 10

Timing Information:

Preparation	Cooking	Total Time
50 mins	30 mins	1 hr 20 mins

Nutritional Information:

Calories	371 kcal
Carbohydrates	24.3 g
Cholesterol	57 mg
Fat	24.9 g
Fiber	1.3 g
Protein	11.9 g
Sodium	467 mg

* Percent Daily Values are based on a 2,000 calorie diet.

DUMPLINGS

Ingredients:

- 4 C. all-purpose flour
- 2 tsps baking powder
- 1 1/2 tsps salt
- 1/2 C. butter
- 1/2 C. cold water
- 1 C. vegetable oil for frying

Directions:

- Get a bowl mix evenly some flour, salt, and baking powder.
- Add butter and continue mixing until it becomes small balls like peas.
- Add 1 tbsp of water to the flour continually until you have dough.
- Shape the dough into large balls.
- Form multiple biscuit shapes from your dough.

- Get a frying pan hot with oil. Fry biscuits for 3 min per side.
- After frying remove excess oil.
- Enjoy.

Servings: 6

Timing Information:

Preparation	Cooking	Total Time
10 mins	10 mins	20 mins

Nutritional Information:

Calories	472 kcal
Carbohydrates	64 g
Cholesterol	41 mg
Fat	19.8 g
Fiber	2.3 g
Protein	8.8 g
Sodium	855 mg

* Percent Daily Values are based on a 2,000 calorie diet.

Easier Jamaican Curry Chicken

Ingredients:

- 3 tbsps vegetable oil
- 1 (3 lb) chicken, cut into pieces
- 1 large onion, diced
- 6 cloves garlic, minced
- 4 large potatoes - peeled and cubed
- 2 tbsps salt
- 1/4 C. Jamaican curry powder
- hot pepper sauce to taste

Directions:

- Get a frying pan hot with oil.
- Stir fry garlic, onions, and chicken. Until chicken is brown. For around 7 mins.
- Add curry powder, salt, and potatoes, to chicken. Stir-fry for 1 min.

- Add water to the halfway mark of your chicken. Place a lid on the pan. Set heat to low.
- Let contents lightly boil for 35 to 41 mins.
- Enjoy after cooling.

NOTE: Use a chili sauce for extra flavor.

Servings: 8

Timing Information:

Preparation	Cooking	Total Time
25 mins	35 mins	1 hr

Nutritional Information:

Calories	574 kcal
Carbohydrates	36.6 g
Cholesterol	128 mg
Fat	31.4 g
Fiber	5.5 g
Protein	36.1 g
Sodium	1908 mg

* Percent Daily Values are based on a 2,000 calorie diet.

Jamaican Bread II

(Banana)

Ingredients
- 2 tbsps unsalted butter, softened
- 2 tbsps cream cheese
- 1 C. white sugar
- 1 egg
- 2 C. all-purpose flour
- 2 tsps baking powder
- 1/2 tsp baking soda
- 1/8 tsp salt
- 1 C. mashed overripe bananas
- 1/2 C. milk
- 2 tbsps dark rum, or rum flavoring
- 1/2 tsp lime zest
- 2 tsps lime juice
- 1 tsp vanilla extract
- 1/4 C. diced toasted pecans
- 1/4 C. flaked coconut

Glaze:
- 1/4 C. brown sugar

- 2 tsps unsalted butter
- 2 tsps lime juice
- 2 tsps dark rum, or rum flavoring
- 2 tbsps diced toasted pecans
- 2 tbsps flaked coconut

Directions
- Coat 2 bread pans with oil and then set your oven to 375 degrees before doing anything else.
- Get a bowl and combine your cream and 2 tbsps of butter. Then gradually add in your sugar and mix everything together.
- Now add in the eggs.
- Get a 2nd bowl, combine: salt, flour, baking soda, and baking powder.
- Get a 3rd bowl, mix: vanilla extract, bananas, lime juice, milk, lime zest, and rum (2 tbsps).
- Now combine all three bowls gradually then mix the contents very well for at least 5 mins.
- Now add 1/4 a C. of the following: coconut flakes and pecans.

- Evenly divide the mix between your bread pans and cook them for 65 mins in the oven.
- Get the following gently boiling while stirring: 2 tbsps rum, brown sugar, lime juice, and the rest of the butter.
- Cook this mix for about 2 mins until the sugar is fully incorporated. Shut the heat and add 2 tbsps of coconut and 2 tbsps pecans.
- Spread the glaze over your bread and then serve.
- Enjoy.

Servings: 24

Timing Information:

Preparation	Cooking	Total Time
45 m	1 h	1 h 45 m

Nutritional Information:

Calories	131 kcal
Fat	3.8 g
Carbohydrates	22g
Protein	1.9 g
Cholesterol	13 mg
Sodium	92 mg

* Percent Daily Values are based on a 2,000 calorie diet.

Jamaican Pork

Ingredients
- 3/4 C. water
- 1/3 C. lemon juice
- 1/3 C. diced onion
- 1 tbsp packed brown sugar
- 1 tbsp diced green onion
- 1 tbsp canola oil
- 3/4 tsp salt
- 3/4 tsp ground allspice
- 3/4 tsp ground cinnamon
- 3/4 tsp ground black pepper
- 1/2 tsp dried thyme, crushed
- 1/4 tsp cayenne pepper, or to taste
- 6 lean pork chops, 1/2 inch thick

Directions
- Blend the following with a blender: cayenne, water, thyme, onion, black pepper, lemon juice, brown sugar, cinnamon, green onions, allspice, oil, and salt.
- Place half a C. to the side.

- Mix the brown sugar mix with the pork in a bowl.
- Now place a lid on the bowl and place the contents in the fridge throughout the night.
- Get your grill hot and oil the grate.
- Grill your pork for 6 mins then flip the pork and cook for 7 more mins.
- Baste the pork with the reserved marinade and serve.
- Enjoy.

Servings: 6

Timing Information:

Preparation	Cooking	Total Time
15 m	10 m	12 h 30 m

Nutritional Information:

Calories	235 kcal
Fat	9.3 g
Carbohydrates	5g
Protein	31.4 g
Cholesterol	81 mg
Sodium	343 mg

* Percent Daily Values are based on a 2,000 calorie diet.

Caribbean Cranberry Spread

Ingredients
- 2 (12 oz.) packages fresh cranberries
- 1 orange, zested
- 3 cinnamon sticks
- 2 C. orange juice
- 2 C. packed brown sugar

Directions
- Get the following boiling: water, brown sugar, cranberries, orange juice, orange zest, and cinnamon.
- Once the mix is boiling, set the heat to low and gently cook everything for 65 mins. Ensure the mix is thick and sweet, if not, add some more sugar.
- Pour everything into a mason jar and place the contents in the fridge.
- Enjoy.

Servings: 24

Timing Information:

Preparation	Cooking	Total Time
10 m	1 h 15 m	1 h 25 m

Nutritional Information:

Calories	93 kcal
Fat	0.1 g
Carbohydrates	23.9g
Protein	0.3 g
Cholesterol	0 mg
Sodium	6 mg

* Percent Daily Values are based on a 2,000 calorie diet.

Shrimp Kebabs

Ingredients
- 1/3 C. lime juice
- 1/3 C. honey
- 1 tsp soy sauce
- 1 tsp vegetable oil
- 2 tbsps Jamaican jerk seasoning
- 3 dashes hot pepper sauce
- salt and pepper to taste
- 2 lbs large shrimp, peeled and deveined
- 12 wooden skewers, soaked in water for 1 hour

Directions
- Get a bowl, combine: jerk spice, oil, hot sauce, lime juice, pepper, soy sauce, salt, and honey.
- Combine in the shrimp and place a covering of plastic over the bowl. Place everything in the fridge for 1 to 2 hours then stake the shrimp onto the skewers, then

coat each one with nonstick spray.
- Now get your grill hot and place some oil on the grate.
- Grill your kebabs for 6 mins then flip each one and grill for 6 more mins.
- Enjoy.

Servings: 6

Timing Information:

Preparation	Cooking	Total Time
20 m	10 m	1 h 30 m

Nutritional Information:

Calories	235 kcal
Fat	3.5 g
Carbohydrates	19.5g
Protein	31 g
Cholesterol	230 mg
Sodium	825 mg

* Percent Daily Values are based on a 2,000 calorie diet.

Caribbean Style Fettuccine

Ingredients
- 1 tbsp olive oil
- 2 skinless, boneless chicken breast halves - cubed
- 1 (8 oz.) can pineapple tidbits with juice
- 1/4 C. shredded coconut
- 2 tbsps brown sugar
- 1 tsp jerk seasoning mix
- 1/2 tsp ground cinnamon
- 1/2 tsp chili powder
- 1/2 tsp crushed red pepper flakes
- salt and ground black pepper to taste
- 4 oz. dry fettuccine

Directions
- Stir fry your chicken in olive oil, until fully done, for about 12 mins.
- Now add in: pepper, coconut, pineapples and liquid, pepper

flakes, brown sugar, chili powder, salt, jerk spice, and cinnamon.
- Get this mix boiling, set the heat to low, and gently cook everything for 16 mins.
- At the same time, boil your pasta in water and salt for 9 mins, then remove all the liquids.
- Combine the pasta with the chicken and stir the contents.
- Enjoy.

Servings: 2

Timing Information:

Preparation	Cooking	Total Time
15 m	25 m	40 m

Nutritional Information:

Calories	628 kcal
Fat	19.5 g
Carbohydrates	79.2g
Protein	35.1 g
Cholesterol	69 mg
Sodium	298 mg

* Percent Daily Values are based on a 2,000 calorie diet.

Fruity Rum Cake

Ingredients
- 2 C. butter
- 2 C. white sugar
- 9 eggs
- 1/4 C. white rum (optional)
- 1 tbsp lime juice
- 1 tsp vanilla extract
- 1 tbsp almond extract
- 1 grated zest of one lime
- 2 lbs diced dried mixed fruit
- 2 C. red wine
- 1 C. dark molasses
- 2 1/2 C. all-purpose flour
- 3 tsps baking powder
- 1/2 tsp ground nutmeg
- 1/2 tsp ground allspice
- 1/2 tsp ground cinnamon
- 1 pinch salt

Directions
- Coat two bread pans with oil and flour, then set your oven to 350

degrees before doing anything else.
- Get a bowl, combine: sugar and butter. Mix the contents until smooth, then add in: lime zest, molasses, eggs, almond extract, wine, rum, vanilla, mixed fruit, and lime juice.
- Get a 2nd bowl, combine: salt, flour, cinnamon, baking powder, allspice, and nutmeg.
- Combine both bowls evenly and mix for 5 mins.
- Evenly divide your mix between the pans and cook them in the oven for 1.5 hours.
- Enjoy.

Servings: 12

Timing Information:

Preparation	Cooking	Total Time
20 m	1 h 30 m	1 h 50 m

Nutritional Information:

Calories	862 kcal
Fat	35.1 g
Carbohydrates	124.2g
Protein	9.6 g
Cholesterol	221 mg
Sodium	418 mg

* Percent Daily Values are based on a 2,000 calorie diet.

West Indian Egg Noodle Low Mein

Ingredients
- 1 (8 oz.) package egg noodles
- 1/2 C. vegetable oil for frying, or as needed
- 2 chili peppers, diced
- 1 onion, finely diced
- 1 clove garlic, minced
- 1 (1 1/2 inch) piece ginger root, cut into strips
- 5 tbsps dark soy sauce
- 2 skinless, boneless chicken breast halves, diced
- 1 green bell pepper, cut into strips
- 2 large carrots, cut into strips
- 1 tbsp ground white pepper
- 5 tbsps dark soy sauce
- 1/4 C. diced fresh cilantro, or more to taste
- salt to taste (optional)
- 4 green onions, finely diced

Directions

- Boil your noodles in water and salt for 8 mins then remove all the liquids.
- Begin to stir fry: ginger, chili peppers, garlic, and onions in veggie oil for 4 mins. Combine in 5 tbsps of soy sauce and cook the contents for 2 more mins. Now add in the chicken and continue stirring and frying for 9 mins until the chicken is fully done.
- Combine in the carrots and bell peppers.
- Cook the veggies for 6 mins.
- Now pour your pasta into the chicken and toss the mix. Add in cilantro, white pepper, and 5 additional tbsps of soy sauce.
- Cook everything 3 more mins until the soy sauce is hot and now serve the mix with some green onions as a garnish.
- Enjoy.

Servings: 4

Timing Information:

Preparation	Cooking	Total Time
35 m	25 m	1 h

Nutritional Information:

Calories	380 kcal
Fat	7 g
Carbohydrates	55.5g
Protein	24.6 g
Cholesterol	81 mg
Sodium	2328 mg

* Percent Daily Values are based on a 2,000 calorie diet.

Jamaican Wings II

Ingredients
- 1/2 yellow onion, diced
- 1/2 C. green onions, sliced
- 6 cloves garlic
- 3 habanero peppers, seeded and diced
- 2 tbsps fresh thyme leaves
- 1 tbsp kosher salt
- 2 tsps ground black pepper
- 2 tsps ground allspice
- 1 tsp dried thyme
- 1/2 tsp ground cinnamon
- 1/2 tsp ground cumin
- 1/2 tsp freshly grated nutmeg
- 2 tbsps vegetable oil
- 3 tbsps soy sauce
- 2 tbsps brown sugar
- 1/3 C. lime juice
- 3 lbs chicken wing drumettes
- cooking spray

Directions

- Process the following with a food processor: lime juice, yellow onion, brown sugar, green onions, soy sauce, garlic, veggie oil, habaneros, nutmeg, fresh thyme, cumin, salt, cinnamon, black pepper, dry thyme, and allspice.
- Coat your chicken with this mix in a bowl and place a cover over everything. Chill the contents for 8 hours.
- Now cover a casserole dish with foil and nonstick spray then set your oven to 450 degrees before doing anything else.
- Layer your chicken in the dish and cook the meat in the oven for 30 mins.
- Now coat the chicken with half of the marinade and flip each piece.
- Continue cooking for 17 more mins before adding the rest of the marinade flipping the chicken again.
- Cook the chicken for 15 more mins.

- Enjoy.

Servings: 6

Timing Information:

Preparation	Cooking	Total Time
15 m	50 m	9 h 10 m

Nutritional Information:

Calories	253 kcal
Fat	15.9 g
Carbohydrates	11.4g
Protein	16.6 g
Cholesterol	48 mg
Sodium	1463 mg

* Percent Daily Values are based on a 2,000 calorie diet.

Sweet and Spicy Wings

Ingredients
- 2 tbsps baking powder
- 1 tbsp kosher salt
- 1 tsp freshly ground black pepper
- 1 tsp smoked paprika
- 2 1/2 lbs chicken wing sections

Honey Sriracha Glaze:
- 1/3 C. honey
- 1/3 C. sriracha sauce
- 1 tbsp seasoned rice vinegar
- 1/4 tsp sesame oil
- 1 pinch sesame seeds, or as desired

Directions
- Cover a casserole dish with foil and nonstick spray then set your oven to 425 degrees before doing anything else.
- Get a bowl, combine: paprika, baking powder, black pepper, and salt.

- Add in the chicken and toss everything to coat the wings.
- Layer the chicken in the dish and cook the meat in the oven for 25 mins then flip each piece and cook for 22 more mins.
- Flip one last time and cook for 10 more mins.
- Now get a 2nd bowl, combine: sesame oil, honey, rice vinegar, and sriracha. Mix everything together until the mix is evenly combined then add your chicken to the bowl and toss the wings in the sauce.
- Lay your chicken onto a serving dish and pour any remaining sauce over them.
- Enjoy.

Servings: 4

Timing Information:

Preparation	Cooking	Total Time
5 m	55 m	1 h

Nutritional Information:

Calories	315 kcal
Fat	14.3 g
Carbohydrates	28.7g
Protein	19.3 g
Cholesterol	59 mg
Sodium	3152 mg

* Percent Daily Values are based on a 2,000 calorie diet.

Cod Fritters

Ingredients
- 6 oz. dried salted cod fish, soaked for 8 hours in water
- cold water, to cover
- 1 C. all-purpose flour
- 1 tsp baking powder
- 2 tsps ground black pepper
- 1/2 C. water
- 1 large tomato, diced
- 2 green onions, diced
- vegetable oil for frying

Directions
- Take out any bones and skin from your fish then shred it.
- Get a bowl, combine: fish, pepper, green onions, half a C. of water, flour, diced tomatoes, and baking powder.
- Get your oil hot, about 1/2 an inch of it, in a pan and cook tbsps dollops of the fish mix for 6 mins per side.

- Place everything on some paper towels to drain.
- Continue frying all your mix in tbsp dollops.
- Enjoy your fritters.

Servings: 6

Timing Information:

Preparation	Cooking	Total Time
1 h	20 m	1 d 1 h 20 m

Nutritional Information:

Calories	232 kcal
Fat	8.3 g
Carbohydrates	18.1g
Protein	20.4 g
Cholesterol	43 mg
Sodium	2079 mg

* Percent Daily Values are based on a 2,000 calorie diet.

Jamaican Pastries

Ingredients

Pastry:
- 2 C. all-purpose flour
- 1 tsp salt
- 1/4 C. cold butter, cut into 1/2 inch pieces
- 3 tbsps shortening, chilled and diced
- 1 egg, beaten
- 1 tbsp ice-cold water

Filling:
- 3 very ripe (black) plantains
- 1/4 C. white sugar
- 1 tsp vanilla extract
- 1 tsp grated nutmeg
- 2 drops red food coloring (optional)
- 1 egg white, beaten
- white sugar, garnish

Directions

- Get a bowl mix: butter, salt, and flour.
- Then add the water and eggs.
- Combine everything until you have a dough.
- Place a covering over the bowl and put everything in the fridge for 4 hours.
- Now remove the skins on your plantains and cut each one into 3 pieces.
- Now simmer the pieces in a bit of water for 12 mins then remove the water and place everything in a bowl with: red food coloring, sugar, nutmeg, and vanilla.
- Mash everything together and let the mix rest.
- Now set your oven to 350 degrees before doing anything else.
- Coat a cutting board with flour and then roll out your dough to 1/4 of an inch.
- Use a large cookie cutter to make circles and add a bit of plantain mix to the middle of each dough

circle then fold them to form a semi-circle.
- Layer everything in a casserole dish coated with nonstick spray then brush each pastry with whisked egg whites and then top each one with sugar.
- Cook the pastries in the oven for 27 mins then let them sit for 10 mins before serving.
- Enjoy.

Servings: 25

Timing Information:

Preparation	Cooking	Total Time
25 m	40 m	7 h 5 m

Nutritional Information:

Calories	107 kcal
Fat	3.8 g
Carbohydrates	17.1g
Protein	1.7 g
Cholesterol	12 mg
Sodium	112 mg

* Percent Daily Values are based on a 2,000 calorie diet.

Maggie's Easy Caribbean Lime Mahi Mahi

Ingredients
- 2 lbs mahi mahi fillets
- 1/2 C. dark rum
- 1/2 C. fresh lime juice
- 2 onion, sliced into thin rings
- 1 lemon, sliced
- 2 tsps dried oregano
- 4 tbsps butter
- ground black pepper to taste

Directions
- Layer your pieces of fish in a casserole dish then top them with lime juice and rum.
- Put a piece of onion on each and place a covering of plastic around the entire dish.
- Chill the contents in the fridge for 5 hrs.
- Now set your oven to 325 degrees before doing anything else.

- Discard about 75% of the liquid in the dish and top your pieces of fish with black pepper and oregano.
- Dot each filet with a piece of butter then cook the mix in the oven for 25 mins. Plate the fish with some lemon pieces and cooked onions as a garnish.
- Enjoy.

Servings: 4

Timing Information:

Preparation	Cooking	Total Time
15 m	25 m	5 h

Nutritional Information:

Calories	400 kcal
Fat	13.3 g
Carbohydrates	11.1g
Protein	43.3 g
Cholesterol	197 mg
Sodium	286 mg

* Percent Daily Values are based on a 2,000 calorie diet.

West Indian Potatoes

Ingredients
- 1/2 lb peeled and deveined medium shrimp
- 1 tbsp white wine vinegar
- 1 tbsp seafood seasoning (such as Old Bay(R))
- 1 tsp ground cumin
- 2 tbsps olive oil
- 1 small onion, minced
- 1 celery stalk, minced
- 1 small carrot, minced
- 1/2 red bell pepper, minced
- 1/4 scotch bonnet chili pepper, minced
- 2 cloves garlic, minced
- 1 tbsp curry powder
- 1/2 C. water
- 2 potatoes, cubed
- 2 C. hot water
- 1 C. frozen French cut green beans, thawed
- 1 bunch fresh cilantro leaves, diced

- salt and pepper to taste

Directions
- Get bowl, mix: cumin, shrimp, seafood seasoning, and white wine vinegar.
- Stir fry your onions in oil for 9 mins then add in: bonnet pepper, celery, bell peppers, and carrots.
- Cook the mix for 7 more mins then add the garlic and cook the mix for 2 more mins.
- Get a bowl, combine: half a C. of water and the curry powder.
- Now combine the potatoes and curry mix with the onions and cook everything for 4 mins.
- Add in 2 C. of hot water and get everything boiling.
- Mix in your green beans and reduce the heat.
- Let the contents gently cook for 22 mins then add the shrimp and continue cooking until they are done for about 6 more mins.

- Add some pepper, salt, and cilantro.
- Enjoy.

Servings: 2

Timing Information:

Preparation	Cooking	Total Time
30 m	40 m	1 h 10 m

Nutritional Information:

Calories	499 kcal
Fat	16.9 g
Carbohydrates	57.6g
Protein	30.3 g
Cholesterol	173 mg
Sodium	1073 mg

* Percent Daily Values are based on a 2,000 calorie diet.

West Indian Hot Habanero Sauce

Ingredients
- 15 habanero peppers, diced
- 1 small mango - peeled, seeded, and cut into chunks
- 1 onion, roughly diced
- 3 green onions, roughly diced
- 2 cloves garlic, roughly diced
- 1 1/2 C. distilled white vinegar
- 2 limes, juiced
- 2 tbsps vegetable oil
- 1/4 C. dry mustard powder
- 1 tbsp salt
- 1 tsp curry powder
- 1/2 tsp grated lime zest

Directions
- Blend the following: garlic, peppers, green onions, mango, and regular onions.
- Blend the mix for 3 mins then add: veggie oil, lime juice, and vinegar.

- Blend everything until smooth then add: lime zest, dry mustard, curry powder, and salt.
- Continue blending until the mix is smooth.
- Then enter everything into mason jars to use with other recipes.
- Keep the mix in the fridge.
- Enjoy.

NOTE: Use this hot sauce for stews and over any meat. If you want to make any sandwich new and refreshing add a bit of this mix to one side of the bread!

Servings: 100

Timing Information:

Preparation	Cooking	Total Time
30 m		30 m

Nutritional Information:

Calories	7 kcal
Fat	0.4 g
Carbohydrates	0.7g
Protein	0.2 g
Cholesterol	0 mg
Sodium	70 mg

* Percent Daily Values are based on a 2,000 calorie diet.

Bok Choy from Trinidad

Ingredients
- 2 1/2 lbs bone-in chicken pieces
- 2 tbsps garlic powder
- 1 tbsp sea salt
- 1 tbsp cayenne pepper
- 1 (.18 oz.) packet sazon seasoning
- 2 tbsps white sugar
- 3 bok choy stalks, diced

Directions
- Get a bowl, combine: sazon, garlic powder, cayenne, and salt.
- Add in the chicken and stir the mix to evenly coat the meat.
- Now for 5 mins get your Dutch oven hot. Then pour in your sugar and let it cook, while stirring, until it becomes brown.
- Add in your chicken, place a lid on the pot, and cook everything for 27 mins. Take off the lid and continue cooking for 17 more mins.

- Now add the bok choy and cook for a few more mins until it's soft.
- Enjoy.

Servings: 6

Timing Information:

Preparation	Cooking	Total Time
15 m	45 m	1 h

Nutritional Information:

Calories	515 kcal
Fat	43.5 g
Carbohydrates	7.2g
Protein	22.6 g
Cholesterol	88 mg
Sodium	1090 mg

* Percent Daily Values are based on a 2,000 calorie diet.

Caribbean Stew

Ingredients
- 1 (4 lb) whole chicken, cut into pieces
- 3 tbsps finely diced green onion
- 3 tbsps diced fresh cilantro
- 1 tsp minced garlic
- 1 tsp diced onion
- 1 tsp salt
- 1/2 tsp ground black pepper
- 1 tbsp vegetable oil
- 1/4 C. brown sugar
- 1 C. water
- 1/2 C. canned coconut milk (optional)
- 1 tsp red pepper flakes (optional)
- 2 tbsps ketchup
- 1 tbsp butter

Directions
- Top your chicken with: pepper, green onions, salt, cilantro, onions, and garlic. Place a lid on

- the bowl, and let the contents chill in the fridge for 1 hr.
- Grab a saucepan and get your veggie oil hot.
- Add in the sugar and heat it until the sugar turns brown.
- Make sure to stir the mix while heating.
- Once the sugar is brown add in your chicken and sear them.
- Make sure you consistently stir.
- Now place a lid on the pot and cook everything for 3 mins.
- Now add in 1 C. of water, pepper flakes, and coconut milk.
- Take off the lid and cook the mix for 12 mins then add the butter and ketchup.
- Simmer the contents for 25 mins and then add some more salt and pepper.
- When plating your chicken liberally top it with the liquids in the pan.
- Enjoy.

Servings: 8

Timing Information:

Preparation	Cooking	Total Time
15 m	30 m	1 h 15 m

Nutritional Information:

Calories	310 kcal
Fat	20.9 g
Carbohydrates	8.7g
Protein	21.5 g
Cholesterol	65 mg
Sodium	404 mg

* Percent Daily Values are based on a 2,000 calorie diet.

Port of Spain Chicken

Ingredients
- 1 1/2 tbsps fresh lime juice
- 2 fluid oz. rum
- 1 tbsp brown sugar
- 1/4 tsp cayenne pepper
- 1/4 tsp ground clove
- 1/2 tsp ground cinnamon
- 1/2 tsp ground ginger
- 1 tsp black pepper
- 1/2 tsp salt
- 1/2 tsp dried thyme leaves
- 1 (3 lb) whole chicken
- 1 tbsp vegetable oil

Directions
- Set your oven to 325 degrees before doing anything else.
- Get a bowl, combine: thyme leaves, cayenne, salt, clove, pepper, cinnamon, and ginger.
- Now top your pieces of chicken with oil then combine them with the dry mix.

- Evenly coat the chicken with the spices and layer them in a pan for roasting.
- Cook the meat in the oven for 1.5 hours.
- Try to baste the chicken every 15 mins.
- Enjoy.

Servings: (4 total)

Timing Information:

Preparation	Cooking	Total Time
15 m	1 h 30 m	1 h 45 m

Nutritional Information:

Calories	508 kcal
Fat	29.1 g
Carbohydrates	4.8g
Protein	46.1 g
Cholesterol	146 mg
Sodium	432 mg

* Percent Daily Values are based on a 2,000 calorie diet.

Spanish Caribbean Beef

Ingredients
- 1 (8 oz.) can canned tomato sauce
- 1/4 C. sofrito sauce
- 1 (.18 oz.) packet sazon seasoning
- 1 tbsp adobo seasoning
- 1/2 tsp dried oregano
- salt to taste
- 2 lbs beef stew meat
- 2 C. peeled, cubed potatoes
- 1 C. water

Directions
- Get the following boiling in a saucepan: salt, tomato sauce, oregano, sofrito, adobo, and sazon.
- Once the mix is boiling set the heat to a lower level and cook the contents for 6 mins.
- Now add in the beef and some water to submerge it.
- Place a lid on the pot and cook everything for 65 mins.

- Now combine in the potatoes and continue cooking for 35 more mins.
- Enjoy.

Servings: (4 total)

Timing Information:

Preparation	Cooking	Total Time
15 m	2 h	2 h 15 m

Nutritional Information:

Calories	677 kcal
Fat	46.5 g
Carbohydrates	18.5g
Protein	44.6 g
Cholesterol	155 mg
Sodium	971 mg

* Percent Daily Values are based on a 2,000 calorie diet.

Jamaican Salad

Ingredients

- 2 skinless, boneless chicken breast halves
- 1/2 C. teriyaki marinade sauce
- 2 tomatoes, seeded and diced
- 1/2 C. diced onion
- 2 tsps minced jalapeno pepper
- 2 tsps diced fresh cilantro
- 1/4 C. Dijon mustard
- 1/4 C. honey
- 1 1/2 tbsps white sugar
- 1 tbsp vegetable oil
- 1 1/2 tbsps cider vinegar
- 1 1/2 tsps lime juice
- 3/4 lb mixed salad greens
- 1 (8 oz.) can pineapple chunks, drained
- 4 C. corn tortilla chips

Directions

- Get a bowl, combine: teriyaki and chicken.

- Place a covering on the bowl, and put everything in the fridge for 3 hrs.
- Get a 2nd bowl, combine: cilantro, tomatoes, jalapenos, and onions.
- Place a covering on this bowl as well and chill the contents in the fridge also.
- Get a 3rd bowl, mix: lime juice, mustard, vinegar, honey, oil, and sugar.
- Get the mix nice and smooth then place a covering on the bowl and place it in the fridge too.
- Now get your grill hot and oil the grate. Cook the chicken for 9 mins per side.
- Layer your greens on a serving plate then top them with some of the contents from 2nd bowl, then add some pineapple and crushed tortilla chips.
- Add your preferred amount of grilled chicken then top everything liberally with the sweet sauce in the 3rd bowl.

- Enjoy.

Servings: (4 total)

Timing Information:

Preparation	Cooking	Total Time
30 m	15 m	2 h 45 m

Nutritional Information:

Calories	443 kcal
Fat	11.3 g
Carbohydrates	68.8g
Protein	18.9 g
Cholesterol	34 mg
Sodium	1561 mg

* Percent Daily Values are based on a 2,000 calorie diet.

Shrimp Salad

Ingredients
- 1 tbsp vegetable oil
- 2 tbsps minced fresh ginger root
- 2 limes, juiced
- 2 cloves garlic, minced
- 1 tbsp soy sauce
- 1/2 tsp white sugar
- 1/2 tsp crushed red pepper flakes
- 2 lbs large cooked shrimp, peeled, tails on
- 1/2 C. diced fresh cilantro

Directions
- Get a bowl, combine: red pepper, oil, sugar, ginger, soy sauce, lime juice, and garlic.
- Combine in the shrimp and place a covering on the bowl.
- Chill the mix in the fridge for 2 hrs then stir it once after 1 hr.
- Enjoy.

Servings: (8 total)

Timing Information:

Preparation	Cooking	Total Time
10 m		1 h 10 m

Nutritional Information:

Calories	138 kcal
Fat	3.1 g
Carbohydrates	2.9g
Protein	24.1 g
Cholesterol	221 mg
Sodium	369 mg

* Percent Daily Values are based on a 2,000 calorie diet.

Spicy Coconut Chicken Bake

Ingredients
- 4 skinless, boneless chicken breasts
- 1 tsp vegetable oil
- 1 1/2 onions, diced
- 1 red bell pepper, diced
- 1 green bell pepper, diced
- 1 tbsp diced roasted garlic
- 1/2 (14 oz.) can coconut milk
- salt and pepper to taste
- 1 pinch crushed red pepper flakes

Directions
- Set your oven to 425 degrees before doing anything else.
- Stir fry your chicken in veggie oil until browned all over then add the bell peppers and onions.
- Cook the mix until the onions are see-through and then add your coconut milk and garlic.
- Cook the contents for 7 more mins before shutting the heat.

- Add in some pepper flakes, black pepper, and salt.
- Now pour everything into a casserole dish and cook the mix in the oven for 50 mins.
- Enjoy.

Servings: (4 total)

Timing Information:

Preparation	Cooking	Total Time
10 m	1 h	1 h 20 m

Nutritional Information:

Calories	272 kcal
Fat	13.3 g
Carbohydrates	9.2g
Protein	29.4 g
Cholesterol	68 mg
Sodium	87 mg

* Percent Daily Values are based on a 2,000 calorie diet.

Trinidad Chicken and Curry

Ingredients
- 3 tbsps vegetable oil
- 1 (3 lb) chicken, cut into pieces
- 1 large onion, diced
- 6 cloves garlic, minced
- 4 large potatoes - peeled and cubed
- 2 tbsps salt
- 1/4 C. Jamaican curry powder
- hot pepper sauce to taste

Directions
- Stir fry your garlic, onions, and chicken in oil for 7 mins then add in the curry powder, salt, and potatoes.
- Pour in some water to submerge the contents and cook the mix for 45 mins, with a lid on the pot, and a gentle boil with a low to medium level of heat.
- Before serving everything add some hot sauce.

- Enjoy.

Servings: 8

Timing Information:

Preparation	Cooking	Total Time
25 m	35 m	1 h

Nutritional Information:

Calories	574 kcal
Fat	31.4 g
Carbohydrates	36.6g
Protein	36.1 g
Cholesterol	128 mg
Sodium	1908 mg

* Percent Daily Values are based on a 2,000 calorie diet.

Caribbean Rice

Ingredients
- 1 (8 oz.) package dry kidney beans
- 4 tbsps olive oil
- 1 bulb shallot, minced
- 3 cloves garlic, minced
- 1 C. uncooked long grain white rice
- 2 bay leaves
- 1 tsp adobo seasoning (optional)
- 1 tbsp kosher salt
- freshly ground black pepper to taste
- 1/4 tsp ground cloves
- 3 sprigs fresh parsley
- 3 sprigs fresh thyme
- 1 scotch bonnet chili pepper

Directions
- Get your beans boiling in three inches of water.

- Once the mix is boiling set the heat to low and cook them for 90 mins.
- Now remove any leftover liquids and place them to the side.
- Combine some water with liquid so that you have 5 C. of it.
- Now stir fry your garlic and shallots then combine in the beans and cook everything for 4 mins.
- Add your 5 C. of liquid and then the rice.
- Get everything boiling then add: thyme, bay leaves, parsley, adobo, cloves, pepper, salt, and the scotch bonnet pepper.
- Place a lid on the pot and set the heat to low.
- Let the contents gently cook for 22 mins. Then take out the leaves, parsley, and pepper.
- Enjoy.

Servings: 6

Timing Information:

Preparation	Cooking	Total Time
15 m	2 h	2 h 15 m

Nutritional Information:

Calories	341 kcal
Fat	9.9 g
Carbohydrates	52.2g
Protein	11.7 g
Cholesterol	0 mg
Sodium	975 mg

* Percent Daily Values are based on a 2,000 calorie diet.

Pina Colada

Ingredients
- 1 1/2 C. white sugar
- 1 1/2 C. water
- 1 (20 oz.) can canned crushed pineapple, drained
- 1 (13.5 oz.) can coconut milk
- 1/4 C. lime juice

Directions
- Get your sugar and water boiling for about 2 mins while stirring. Then shut the heat.
- Process your pineapple in a blender until smooth then combine them with the following in a bowl: lime juice, syrup (boiled water and sugar), and coconut milk.
- Place the contents in the fridge for 4 hrs then the freeze the mix until slightly frozen to make some Pina coladas.
- Enjoy.

Servings: 8

Timing Information:

Preparation	Cooking	Total Time
25 m		25 m

Nutritional Information:

Calories	284 kcal
Fat	10.3 g
Carbohydrates	50.5g
Protein	1.3 g
Cholesterol	0 mg
Sodium	8 mg

* Percent Daily Values are based on a 2,000 calorie diet.

Fried Conch

Ingredients

Fritters:
- 1 quart oil for frying
- 3/4 C. all-purpose flour
- 1 egg
- 1/2 C. milk
- ground cayenne pepper to taste
- seasoned salt to taste
- salt and pepper to taste
- 1 C. diced conch meat
- 1/2 onion, diced
- 1/2 green bell pepper, diced
- 2 stalks celery, diced
- 2 cloves garlic, diced

Dipping Sauce:
- 2 tbsps ketchup
- 2 tbsps lime juice
- 1 tbsp mayonnaise
- 1 tbsp hot sauce
- salt and pepper to taste

Directions
- Get a bowl, combine: garlic, pepper, celery, milk, bell peppers, salt, onions, flour, seasoned salt, conch, and eggs.
- Mix everything into a smooth batter then drop dollops of the mix in 365 degree oil. Cook the fritters until browned all over then drain them on some paper towels.
- Get a 2nd bowl, combine: pepper, ketchup, salt, lime juice, hot sauce, and mayo.
- Serve your fritters with the spicy mayo mix.
- Enjoy.

Servings: 8

Timing Information:

Preparation	Cooking	Total Time
15 m	20 m	35 m

Nutritional Information:

Calories	220 kcal
Fat	13.6 g
Carbohydrates	14.8g
Protein	9.6 g
Cholesterol	44 mg
Sodium	209 mg

* Percent Daily Values are based on a 2,000 calorie diet.

Brown Rice XXXI

(Easy Jamaican Style)

Ingredients

- 1 tbsp vegetable oil
- 1/2 large onion, sliced
- 1/2 red apple, cored and sliced
- 1 pinch curry powder
- 1 C. water
- 2/3 C. brown rice
- 1 tsp dark molasses or treacle
- 1 small banana, sliced
- 1 tbsp unsweetened flaked coconut

Directions

- Stir fry your apples and onions in oil until the onions are see-through then add in curry.

- Cook everything for 1 more min before pouring in your water, molasses, and rice.
- Get everything boiling before placing a lid on the pot, setting the heat to low, and cooking for 32 mins.
- Add in the bananas and then your coconuts. Get everything hot again then plate the rice.
- Enjoy.

Servings: 8

Timing Information:

Preparation	Cooking	Total Time
10 m	40 m	1 h

Nutritional Information:

Calories	398 kcal
Fat	10.7 g
Carbohydrates	71.6g
Protein	6.1 g
Cholesterol	0 mg
Sodium	11 mg

* Percent Daily Values are based on a 2,000 calorie diet.

Thanks for Reading! Now Let's Try some Sushi and Dump Dinners....

<u>Send the Book!</u>

To grab this **box set** simply follow the link mentioned above, or tap the book cover.

This will take you to a page where you can simply enter your email address and a PDF version of the **box set** will be emailed to you.

I hope you are ready for some serious cooking!

<u>Send the Book!</u>

You will also receive updates about all my new books when they are free.

Also don't forget to like and subscribe on the social networks. I love meeting my readers. Links to all my profiles are below so please click and connect :)

<u>Facebook</u>

<u>Twitter</u>

Come On...
Let's Be Friends :)

I adore my readers and love connecting with them socially. Please follow the links below so we can connect on Facebook, Twitter, and Google+.

Facebook

Twitter

I also have a blog that I regularly update for my readers so check it out below.

My Blog

Can I Ask A Favour?

If you found this book interesting, or have otherwise found any benefit in it. Then may I ask that you post a review of it on Amazon? Nothing excites me more than new reviews, especially reviews which suggest new topics for writing. I do read all reviews and I always factor feedback into my newer works.

So if you are willing to take ten minutes to write what you sincerely thought about this book then please visit our Amazon page and post your opinions.

Again thank you!

INTERESTED IN OTHER EASY COOKBOOKS?

Everything is easy! Check out my Amazon Author page for more great cookbooks:

For a complete listing of all my books please see my author page.

Printed in Great Britain
by Amazon